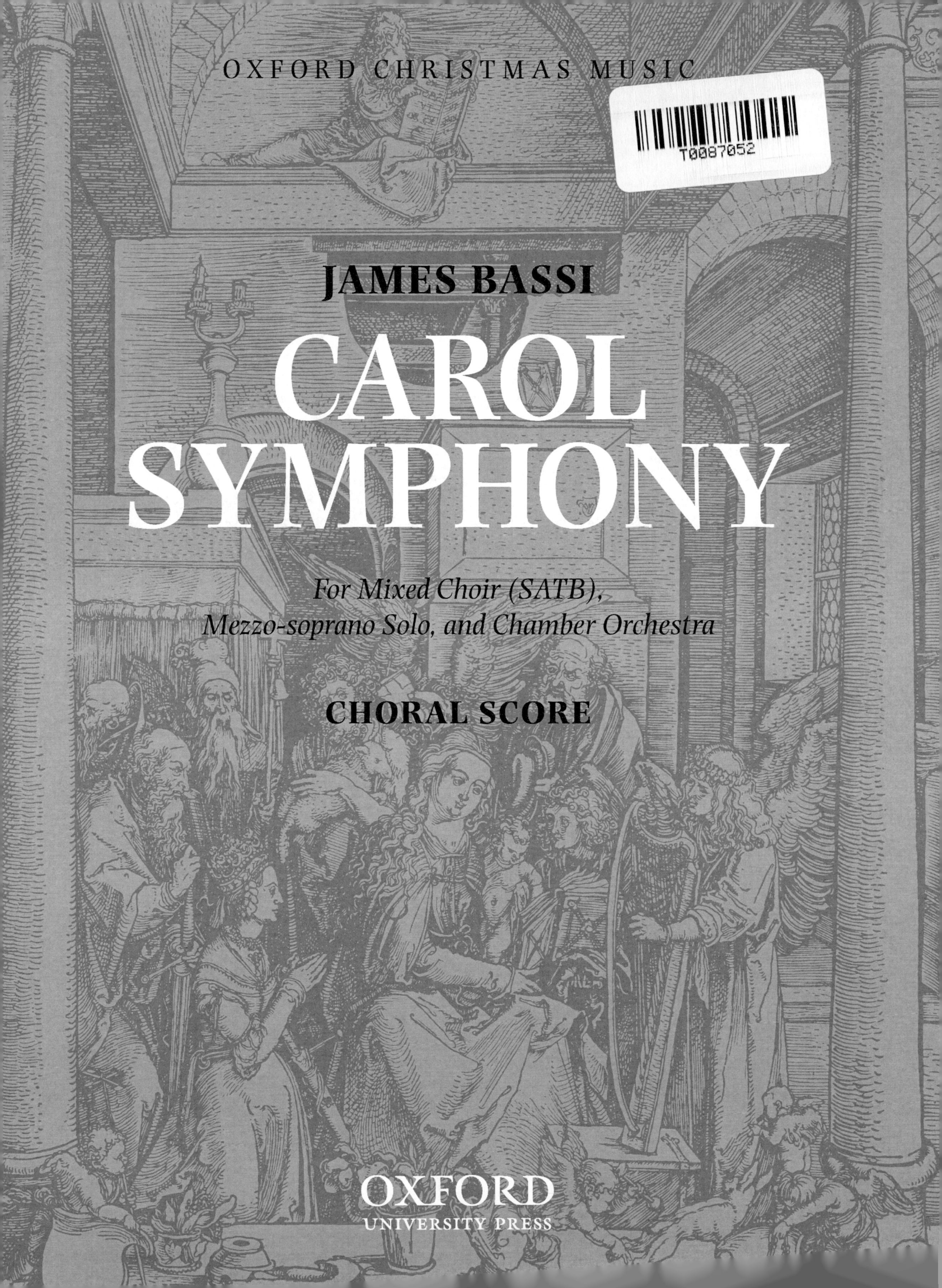

OXFORD CHRISTMAS MUSIC

JAMES BASSI

CAROL SYMPHONY

For Mixed Choir (SATB),
Mezzo-soprano Solo, and Chamber Orchestra

CHORAL SCORE

OXFORD
UNIVERSITY PRESS

JAMES BASSI

CAROL SYMPHONY

For Mixed Choir (SATB),
Mezzo-soprano Solo, and Chamber Orchestra

Duration: approx. 13 minutes

The orchestration of *Carol Symphony* evolved partly out of practicality. My colleague Johnson Flucker, music director at the Cathedral of St. John the Divine in New York City, commissioned me to write a work that could be performed alongside Handel's *Messiah* (Christmas portion) for a holiday concert at the Cathedral. We agreed that I would score the symphony for "Messiah" orchestra, using no additional players or instruments, with the exception of a few extra percussion instruments. For me, one of the more exciting challenges in composing *Carol Symphony* was to create a lush, contemporary orchestration using limited instrumental forces.

The first movement, "Bells," is a fantasia on a popular Ukranian carol melody, to which I have written my own English lyrics. It is an impressionistic piece, by turns melancholy and vigorous.

The second movement, "Hymn," is a more or less strophic setting of the Irish *Wexford Carol*. In my earlier version for choir and organ, Judy Collins originally sang the solo part. The clarity and directness of her singing serves as a guideline for soloists approaching this piece. It does not warrant a full operatic sound; it is closer to the folk tradition in overall presentation. The singer should simply tell the story. Given the low tessitura of the part, and depending on the acoustics involved, I would recommend amplification of the soloist, to achieve an easy balance with the accompanying forces.

The third movement, "Dance," is a kind of rhythmic theme-and-variations on the English carol "Tomorrow Shall Be My Dancing Day." The tune undergoes a series of transformations, appearing in different meters, and never in its original 6/8 version. An orchestral toccata section precedes the spirited finale.

—*James Bassi*

The full score and set of parts (2ob., bn., 2tpt., perc., str.) for *Carol Symphony* are available on rental from the Publisher. A setting of the second movement, *Wexford Carol*, for mezzo-soprano, SATB, and organ, with optional handbells, is offered for sale (0-19-386576-9).

to Johnson Flucker and the Choir
of the Cathedral of St. John the Divine

Carol Symphony

For Mixed Choir (SATB), Mezzo-soprano Solo, and Chamber Orchestra

James Bassi

I. Bells

13
ring in the news,
ten.
Je - sus is born.
poco
16
p
Peace and good will,
songs of His praise,
p
e - cho - ing still,
p legato
ah
p legato
ah

19
dim.
ppp
joy - ous - ly raise.
mp espr.
p
22
B
unis. mp dolce
Glad is the sound, chim -
mp dolce
heard all a - round,
mf
mp
3

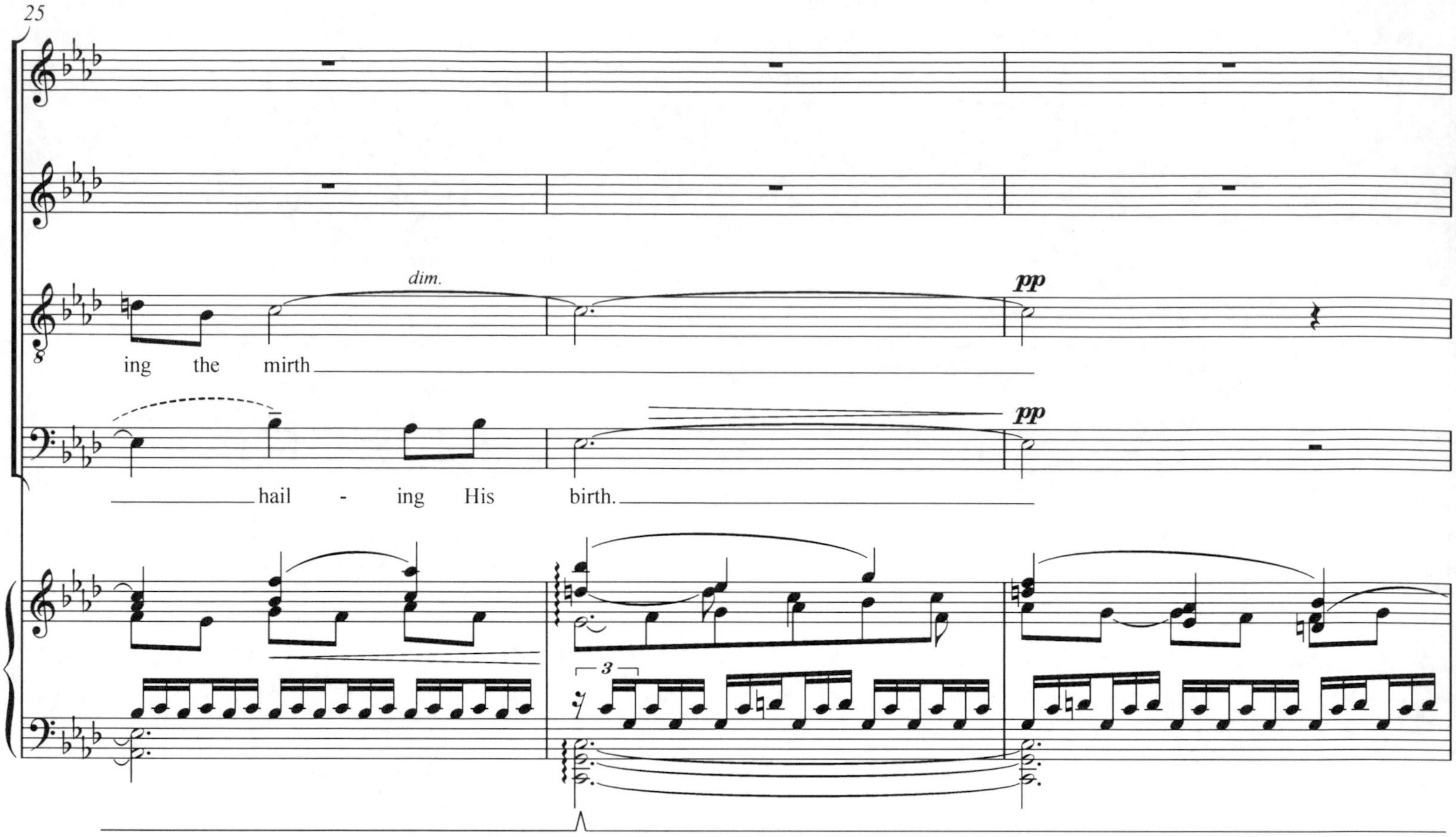
25
dim.
ing the mirth
pp
hail - ing His birth.
pp
3

28
mp
cresc.
Ring strong and clear for all to hear, joy is un - furled through all the
mp
cresc.
Ring strong and clear for all to hear, joy is un - furled through all the
mp
cresc.
Ring strong and clear for all to hear, joy is un - furled through all the
mp
cresc.
Ring strong and clear for all to hear, joy is un - furled through all the
p sub. cresc.
(cresc.)

C
Poco più mosso (♩ = c. 69)
32
S. 1
f
mf legato
world! Ring out the song loud high and long, God's on - ly Son
S. 2
Ring loud and high and long, ring
world! Ring out the song,
world! Ring out the song,
world! Ring
f molto sostenuto
37
più f
free - dom has won. Ring loud and high and long, ring loud and high and
long. Ring out the song loud high and long, ring out the song loud high and long,
ring out loud high and long, ring out loud high and
ring out the song, ring out loud high and
out the song, ring out the song, high and

42
D
stringendo poco a poco
più stringendo
long, ring loud and high and long, ring loud and high and long,
più marc.
ring loud and high and long, ring loud and high and long, ring loud and high and
cresc.
long, ring out the song, ring out,
long, ring out the song, ring out,
long, ring out the song, ring out,
sfz
47
più accel.
più marc.
cresc.
ring loud and high and long, ring!
long, ring loud and high and ring!
ring out, ring out, ring!
ring out, ring out, ring!
ring out, ring out, ring!
ten.
p sub.
cresc. articolato
(cresc.)

E
Allegro, ritmico (♩ = c. 138)
52
ff
mf sub.
f marc., ritmico
58
ritmico ma sostenuto
cresc.
64
F
S. 1&2 tutti
ff
mf
Ring
out
the
bells!
ff marc.

69
ff sub.
Night un - til morn!
mf

74
ff sub.
Je - sus is born!
p
p sub.

79
G
cresc. molto
fff
f
84
mp dolce, molto legato, non cresc.
Ring the
più legato
dim.
mp legato

89
mer - ry bells of Christ - mas,
mp dolce, molto legato, non cresc.
Bells of
mp dolce, molto legato, non cresc.
Ring the mer - ry bells of
mp dolce, molto legato, non cresc.
Ring the mer - ry bells of
94
H
p
ring the mer - ry bells of Christ - - - - mas.
ten.
p
Christ - mas, bells of
ten.
p
Christ - mas, bells of
ten.
p
Christ - mas, bells of
LH
H
dim.
p

100
dim.
Christ - - mas.
Christ - - mas.
Christ - - mas.
mf espr.
108
molto rit.
I
Molto meno mosso, larghetto (♩ = c. 66)
mp
114
p dolce
riten.
mp
pp
Ancora meno mosso, largo (♩ = c. 52)
f
120
dolciss.
p
mp sub.
p
dim.
lunghiss.
lunghiss.
lunghiss.
pp

II. Hymn
(Wexford Carol)

13
(Mezzo-sop. solo)
bear in mind what our good God for us has done, in send-ing his be - lov - ed Son. With
18
B
Ma - ry ho - ly we should pray to God with love this Christ-mas Day; in
S. mp legato
ah
mp sempre legatissimo
22
cresc.
Beth - le - hem up - on that morn, there was a bless - ed Mes - si - ah born.
mp cresc.
Up - on that morn, a bless - ed Mes -

27
C
Poco più mosso
The night be - fore that hap - py tide, the no - ble Vir - gin
dim.
p
si - ah was born.
Poco più mosso
sempre mp, legato, transparent
Sost. Ped.
32
and her guide were long time seek - ing up and down to find a lodg - ing in the town. But
mp
ah
But
Ah, but
cresc.
(Sost. Ped.)

37
mark how all things came to pass: from ev - 'ry door re - pelled, a - las! As
all things came to pass: from ev - 'ry door re - pelled, a - las! As
mark how all things came to pass: from ev - 'ry door re - pelled, a - las! As
re - pelled.
all things came to pass: from ev - 'ry door re - pelled, a - las! As
all things came to pass: from ev - 'ry door re - pelled, As
mf
dim.
(leg.)
42
cresc.
long fore-told, their re-fuge all was but an hum - ble ox - 's stall.
long fore - told, their re-fuge all.
long fore - told, their re-fuge all.
long fore - told, their re-fuge all.
long fore - told, their re-fuge all.
(cresc.)
f
D Maestoso
molto f
molto decresc.

48
rit.
T. 1
mp dolce
Near
T. 2
mp dolce
Near
B.
mp dolce
Near
rit.
ten.
mp
calmando, dim.
ten.
52
E Poco meno mosso
Beth - le - hem did shep - herds keep their flocks of lambs and feed - ing sheep; to
Beth - le - hem did shep - herds keep their flocks of lambs and feed - ing sheep; to
Beth - le - hem did shep - herds keep their flocks of lambs and feed - ing sheep; to
E Poco meno mosso
p legatissimo
56
whom God's an - - gels did ap - pear, which put the shep - - herds
whom God's an - gels did ap - pear, which put the shep - - herds
whom God's an - gels did ap - pear, which put the shep - - herds

59
muovendo
F Poco più mosso
Mezzo-sop. Solo mf
"Pre - pare and go," the angels said, "to Beth - le - hem, be not a-fraid; for
S. p legato
ah
A. p legato
ah
T.
p sub. legato
in great fear. ah
B.
p sub. legato
unis.
in great fear. ah
muovendo
F Poco più mosso
sempre p, dolce, legato
64
cresc. poco a poco
there you'll find, this hap-py morn, a prince-ly babe, sweet Je - sus
ah
With
ah
With
ah
With

G Grandioso
68
Solo
f
born."
S.
f cantabile
Al - le - lu - ia, al - le - lu - -
A.
f cantabile
thank - ful heart and joy - ful mind, the shep - herds went the babe to find, and,
T.
f
thank - ful heart and joy - ful mind, the shep - herds went the babe to find.
B.
f
thank - ful heart and joy - ful mind, the shep - herds went the babe to find.
G
Grandioso
f
72
With -
(add semi-chorus)
ia, al - le - lu - ia. A - - - - - men. With -
(add semi-chorus)
as God's an - gel had fore - told, they did our Sav - iour Christ be - hold. With -
(add semi-chorus)
as God's an - gel had fore - told, our Christ be - hold. With -
as God's an - gel had fore - told, our Christ be - hold. With -

76
H
Solo
in a man - ger he was laid, and by his side the vir-gin maid. At - tend-ing on the
S.
(legato)
cresc.
in a man - ger he was laid, and by his side the vir-gin maid. ah
Semi-Chorus
A.
(legato)
cresc.
in a man - ger he was laid, and by his side the vir-gin maid. ah
T.
(legato)
cresc.
in a man - ger he was laid, and by his side the vir-gin maid. ah
SATB
unis.
più f
cresc.
Full Chorus
in a man - ger he was laid, and by his side the vir-gin maid. At - tend-ing on the
H
con forza
cresc.
81
I
Lord of Life, who came on earth to end all strife.
ff
dim. molto
to Full Chorus
ah
ff
dim. molto
to Full Chorus
ah
ff
dim. molto
to Full Chorus
ah
Lord of Life, who came on earth to end all strife.
I
ff legato
dim. molto
½ Ped.

J Calmato, poco meno mosso
86
Solo
mf dolce, espr.
What our good God for us has done, in
S.
mp legato
ah
A.
mp legato
ah
oo
Full Chorus
T.
mp legato
ah
oo
B.
mp legato
ah
oo
J Calmato, poco meno mosso
p
Full Ped.
91
rit.
ten.
send - ing his be - lov - ed Son.
oo
oo
unis.
unis.
rit.

III. Dance

Allegro energico (♩ = c. 112)
Piano
f marc.
ritmico
Ped.
5
8
mf
Ped.
12
A
S.
f ritmico, poco marc.
To - mor - row shall be my
A.
f ritmico, poco marc.
To - mor - row shall be my
T.
f ritmico, poco marc.
To - mor - row shall be my
B.
f ritmico, poco marc.
To - mor - row shall be my
A
f molto ritmico

15
danc - ing day. I would my true love did so chance to
danc - ing day. I would my true love did so chance to
danc - ing day. I would my true love did so chance to
danc - ing day. I would my true love did so chance to
18
see the le - gend of my play. To call my true love to
see the le - gend of my play. To call my true love to
see the le - gend of my play. To call my true love to
see the le - gend of my play. To call my true love to

21
B
mp
f più legato
my
dance.
Sing,
p sub.
cresc.
24
O
my
love,
O
my
love,
O
my
love.
p
f legato
mf
f articolato, ritmico

28
p dolce, legato
This have I done for my true love.
p dolce, legato
This have I done for my true love.
pp dolce
mf legato, cantabile
32
C
Flowing, legato
quasi p dolce, legato
Then was I born of a
quasi p dolce, legato
Then was I born of a vir - gin
top note
p delicato

36
S.
vir - gin pure. Of her I took flesh - ly sub-stance. Thus was I knit to
A.
pure. Of her I took flesh-ly sub - stance. Thus was I knit to man's na -
poco cresc.
40
to call my true love to my dance, to my dance,
man's na-ture, to call my true love to my dance, to my dance.
ture, to call my true love to my dance, to my dance, to my
mf
(top note)
cresc.
44
D
dance.
p
mf sub.
f sub.
cresc.
f
brillante
marc.

Ritmico
49
T. 1
f ritmico, poco leggiero
In a man - ger laid and
T. 2
f ritmico, poco leggiero
In a man - ger laid and
Ritmico
giocoso
mf sub.
54
wrapped I was. So ve - ry poor, this
wrapped I was. So ve - ry poor, this
59
was my chance, be - tween an ox and a
was my chance, be - tween an ox and a
Ped.

64
E
f
sil - ly poor ass, to call my true love to my
sil - ly poor ass, to call my true
cresc.
Ped.
69
dance, to call my true love to my dance, to my
love to my dance, to call my true love to my
74
F Ritmico, energico
molto
p
dance.
dance.
ff
mf articolato
Ped.

77
f brillante, marc.
f
mp
80
83
G
86
89
S.
f sostenuto ma articolato
To -
A.
f sostenuto ma articolato
To -
T.
f sostenuto ma articolato
To -
B.
f sostenuto ma articolato
To -
fp
cresc.

H
Maestoso e brillante
92
mf
f sub.
mor - row shall be my danc-ing day. I
f sostenuto
tr
(f)
mf
97
would my true love did so chance to

102
S. 1
see the le - gend of my play.
più f
S. 2
see the le - gend of my play.
più f
A. 1
see the le - gend of my play.
più f
A. 2
see the le - gend of my play.
più f
T. 1
see the le - gend of my play.
più f
T. 2
see the le - gend of my play.
più f
B. 1
see the le - gend of my play.
più f
B. 2
see the le - gend of my play.
più f
tr
f sostenuto
più f

106
I
ten.
marc.
To call — my true love, to call my true
To call — my true love, to call
To call — my true love, to call my true
To call — my true love, to call
To call — my true love to call my true
To call — my true love, to call
To call — my true love, to call my true
To call — my true love, to call
I

109
fp
love, to call my true love
fp
my true love, to call my true love
fp
love, to call my true love
fp
my true love, to call my true love
fp
love, to call my true love
fp
my true love, to call my true love
fp
love, to call my true love
fp
my true love, to call my true love
f
mp cresc.
Ped.

113
S.
ff
subito allargando molto
J
a tempo, vivace
unis.
mp
poco a poco cresc.
to my dance!
A.
(unis.)
to my dance!
T.
to my dance!
B.
(unis.)
to my dance!
subito allargando molto
J
a tempo, vivace
f
cresc.
117
fff
mp sub.